Poetic Love Letters to God

La'Kita Stephens

Poetic Love Letters to God

Copyright © 2022 by LaKita Stephens

Honey Tree Publishing

Louisville, Kentucky 40215

First Paperback Edition 2022

All rights reserved. No part of this publication may be reproduced, stored, in a retrieval system, or transmitted in any form by any means, electronic, mechanical, photocopy, recording, or otherwise, without the prior permission of the author.

For contact and/or to place an order, send email to lsstephens95@gmail.com

Editor and Layout Designer: Dr. Tytianna Ringstaff

Cover Designer: Dr. Tytianna Ringstaff and Christopher Ringstaff

Manufactured in the United States of America

ISBN: 978-1-7352516-0-8

Dedication

Dear God,

    Thank you for my life and many blessings. You continue to smile on me with never-ending love. I am not worthy, yet grace and mercy shower me. It is because of your unwavering love that I dedicate this book to you. I pray these words may encourage and enlighten someone along their journey in life.

With all my heart,

La'Kita

Acknowledgement

This book is written with special thanks to my mother Ernestine and great-grandmother Beulah for planting the seed, reading the Bible to me, and being my role models as Christian women.

Rest in peace Granny B. I hope I have made you proud.

Preface

I started writing this book as poems I combined expressing my love for God. Each poem is a reflection of me looking over my life and seeing how God has been there for me. I wrote from personal feelings and accounts of real life, giving the book a feel of being non-fiction.

I hope you will be encouraged by this book and gain strength in your relationship with God. Even if you are not a believer, my desire is that this book will inspire you to feel encouraged. That is the most important thing I want my readers to feel. I want readers to look at their own lives and know that while they may be going through this or that, God is there and to not lose hope.

Table of Inspiration

Because I Love You 1

Without You 3

Help Me Trust You 5

I Called on the Lord 7

Wait Patiently 9

Speak to My Heart 11

Thank You 13

When I Think 15

Keep Pressing On 17

Rejoice 19

I Need You 21

Just When 23

Why Not Serve You? 25

You 27

Still Blessed 29

Just Ask 31

When I Look to You 33

All My Life 35

All to You 37

Safe 39

Watching Over Me 41

Great You Have Been 43

You Forgave Me 45

Learned the Way 47

Final Say 49

Because I Love You

Because I love you, show me your way
Because I love you, I will not stray
Because I love you, I submit to your will
Because I love you, my heart's for you to fill
Because I love you, I give you my trust
Because I love you, I've learned not to rush
Because I love you, I'll never doubt you
Because I love you, my life is brand new
Because I love you, each day is a blessing
Because I love you, there's no time for stressing
Because I love you, you can use me
Because I love you, my life you've set free

Without You

Without you Jesus how could I live
I would be empty with nothing to give

Without you Jesus where would I be
I'd be lost in the dark unable to see

Without you Jesus how could I make it
Your love gives me the strength to take it

Without you Jesus where would I go
You light my path and guidance show

Without you Jesus how could I smile
You fight for me making life worthwhile

Without you Jesus where would I end
In you I have eternal life to begin

Help Me Trust You

I love you Lord
even though I make mistakes
You know what's best for me
when I cry from heartaches
Help me trust you
when life feels upside down
I know you're in control
your spirit always around

I Called on the Lord

I called on the Lord
and
He heard my cry

He forgave my sins
and
I still wonder why

I called on the Lord
and
He answered my prayers

He came right on time
and
relieved my cares

I called on the Lord,
yes...
I called on the Lord

Wait Patiently

Wait patiently on the Lord
Be of good cheer and not discord
Wait patiently for His answer
In any storm He'll give you shelter
Wait patiently for breakthroughs
His plan is perfect for you
Wait patiently for God's timing
He is the wing for your flying
Wait patiently for that glorious day
For your troubles shall soon pass away
Wait patiently on the Lord
Be of good cheer and not discord

Speak to My Heart

Speak to my heart

                                            dear Lord

Show me the way

                                            unless I'd fall

Guide my steps

                                            along this path

I give you my heart

                                            my mind, my all

Thank You

Lord, I thank you for
the sun, the moon, the stars
I thank you cause you've brought me oh so far
I thank you for the days I couldn't see
I'm so glad you know what's best for me

Lord, I thank you for
my health, my strength, my life
I thank you for bringing me through strife
I thank you cause you always know the way
I'm so glad you keep me everyday

Lord, I thank you for
the dark, the clouds, the gloom
I thank you for clearing them and making room
I thank you for your rainbow in the sky
I'm so glad you're with me by and by

When I Think

When I think about my blessings...
When I think about my life...
When I think of how you keep me...

When I think about my sins...
When I think about my faults...
When I think of how you forgive me...

When I think about my days...
When I think about my nights...
When I think of how you guide me...

Keep Pressing On

When trials of life make you feel down
When it seems like no one else is around
When trouble seems to follow you close
When heartache is what hurts you the most
When loneliness and depression set in
When disappointment and disgust begin
When I'm doing well seems hard to say
When you feel like you can't finish the day

    Know that God is in control
    and
    Keep pressing on

Rejoice

Rejoice in the Lord and live **happy**
Rejoice in the Lord and be at **peace**
Rejoice in the Lord and have **faith**
Rejoice in the Lord and live **blessed**
Rejoice in the Lord and be **strong**
Rejoice in the Lord and have **courage**
Rejoice in the Lord and live **thankful**
Rejoice in the Lord and be **comforted**
Rejoice in the Lord and have **assurance**
Rejoice,
Rejoice,
Rejoice in the Lord

I Need You

Whether I'm up or down – I need you
Whether I'm rich or poor – I need you
Whether I'm well or sick – I need you
Whether I'm happy or sad – I need you
Whether I'm rested or tired – I need you
Whether I'm full or hungry – I need you

I need you Lord, I need you

Just When

Just when I was ready to give up
    Just when I said I've had enough
        Just when I seemed all alone
            Just when I had no one to phone
                Just when I couldn't take anymore
                    Just when I worried what was in store...
                        The Lord stepped in

Why Not Serve You?

Who else loves me so?
Who else helps me grow?

What keeps me going?
What keeps blessings flowing?

When I need you, don't you provide?
When I seek you, don't you guide?

Where would I be without you?
Where would life take me to?

Which way could I not find you?
Which day do you not give light to?

Why not serve you?
Why not serve you?

You

When I need you, you are there
When I call you, you answer prayers

When I seek you, you appear
When I trust you, you ease fear

When I hear you, you teach me
When I obey you, you reward me

When I praise you, you fill me
When I honor you, you bless me

Still Blessed

When I'm ready to complain
Remind myself
I'm still blessed

When I'm ready to give up
Remind myself
I'm still blessed

When I'm ready to cry
Remind myself
I'm still blessed

When I'm ready to sulk
Remind myself
I'm still blessed

Still blessed, still blessed
No matter what, I'm still blessed

Just Ask

You told me in your word
Just ask and I'll receive
I hid those words in my heart
Knowing first I must believe
Whether it's a mountain or giant
You're able to make them fall
You give me this same power
When on you I know to call
No matter what I'm facing
I know you're always present
I stand firm forever in faith
Giving you praise, glory, reverence

When I Look to You

When I lift my eyes looking to you,
all things become clear in view
How wonderful and special you are,
guiding me near never far
To be without you I couldn't be,
so glad you're always there for me

When I lift my eyes looking to you,
I feel a love that's so true
How strong the love for your child,
you make each day worthwhile
To be without you I couldn't be,
you mean so very much to me

When I lift my eyes looking to you,
I see and know what to do
How mighty is your hand,
steady leading me to your plan
To be without you I couldn't be,
so glad you know what's best for me

All My Life

All my life
I trusted in you
All my life
I knew your word was true
All my life
through dangers kept me
All my life
heavenly angels did see
All my life
you were my protection
All my life
you've been safe direction
All my life
felt every blessing
All my life
no need for impressing
All my life
tried to do your will
All my life
my cup for you to fill

All to You

All to you I give my life
You keep me from danger and strife
No matter where I go or what I do
I know you will see me through

All to you I lay down it all
You pick me up whenever I fall
No matter where I go or what I do
I know you will see me through

All to you I worship and adore
You supply every need and more
No matter where I go or what I do
I know you will see me through

Safe

You O Lord
are my guiding light
with present help
you keep me in sight

Wherever I go
I feel you near
I walk in faith
with nothing to fear

If I am afraid
you put me at ease
your loving arms
to calm and please

Never alone
I feel your presence
forever my Keeper
I give you reverence

Watching Over Me

Watching over me, watching over me
You are the one Lord, watching over me

Watching over me, watching over me
You are in control Lord, watching over me

Watching over me, watching over me
You are my help Lord, watching over me

Watching over me, watching over me
You are always near Lord, watching over me

Great You Have Been

Great you have been God
Loving me in spite of myself
Through it all I turn to no one else

Great you have been God
Making ways for me
I feel you opening doors I cannot see

Great you have been God
Keeping my mind at peace
Your loving arms make all worry cease

Great you have been God
Providing my every need
Everyday my body and soul you feed

Great you have been God
Guiding me with your hand
On your promises I learned to stand

You Forgave Me

My lack of faith in you
>> Bad decisions, you forgave me
>> Wrong choices, you forgave me

My lack of faith in you
>> Bad attitude, you forgave me
>> Wrong actions, you forgave me

My lack of faith in you
>> Bad habits, you forgave me
>> Wrong situations, you forgave me

My lack of faith in you
>> You forgave me for it all
>> You forgave me for it all

My renewed faith in you

Learned the Way

Can't say my head hasn't been hard –
That some decisions didn't leave scars
That my focus has been free and clear
That I always looked forward not rear
That I stayed trusting never doubting
That my life didn't need rerouting
That I constantly listened and prayed
That I followed the shepherd without stray

There is one thing I can say –
That I finally learned the way

Final Say

Thank you God for having the final say
You open closed doors and make a way
When people say no or turn away
I know you're there to bless my day
I appreciate each and every blessing
It's been you keeping me from stressing
Through ups and downs I can depend
You're with me now until the end

www.ingramcontent.com/pod-product-compliance
Lightning Source LLC
Chambersburg PA
CBHW060412080526
44583CB00012B/547